Bridgestone
BOOKS

World of Mammals

Manatees

by Connie Colwell Miller

Consultant:
Jaime R. Alvarado Bremer, PhD
Departments of Marine Biology and Wildlife and Fisheries Sciences
Texas A&M University
Galveston, Texas

Capstone
press
Mankato, Minnesota

Bridgestone Books are published by Capstone Press,
151 Good Counsel Drive, P.O. Box 669, Mankato, Minnesota 56002.
www.capstonepress.com

Library of Congress Cataloging-in-Publication Data
Miller, Connie Colwell, 1976–
    Manatees / by Connie Colwell Miller.
    p. cm.—(Bridgestone Books. World of mammals)
    Summary: "A brief introduction to manatees, discussing their
characteristics, habitat, life cycle, and predators. Includes a range map,
life cycle illustration, and amazing facts"—Provided by publisher.
    Includes bibliographical references and index.
    ISBN 0-7368-4311-6 (hardcover)
    1. Manatees—Juvenile literature. I. Title. II. Series:World of mammals.
QL737.S63M55 2006
599.55—dc22   2004028437

Editorial Credits

Shari Joffe, editor; Molly Nei, set designer; Biner Design, book designer; Patricia Rasch, illustrator;
    Kelly Garvin, photo researcher; Scott Thoms, photo editor

Photo Credits

Corbis/Brandon D. Cole, 20; Corbis RF/Marty Snyderman, 1
Jeff Rotman, 10
Seapics.com/Doug Perrine, cover, 4, 6, 12, 16
Tom Stack & Associates, Inc./Tom & Therisa Stack, 18

1 2 3 4 5 6 10 09 08 07 06 05

Table of Contents

Manatees

A dark shadow appears under the water. Slowly, a large animal swims by. It looks almost like a hippo with flippers. What is it? It's a manatee.

Manatees are **aquatic mammals**. They spend their lives in the water, but they come to the surface often to breathe air. Like all mammals, manatees have a backbone and are **warm-blooded**. Manatees look like walruses or seals, but they are more closely related to elephants.

◄ Manatees are large, gentle mammals that live in shallow water.

What Manatees Look Like

Manatees have large, smooth bodies. They are gray or brown in color. Adult manatees weigh about 1,000 pounds (453 kilograms). They are usually about 10 feet (3 meters) long.

Manatees have large, paddle-shaped tails and long flippers. They swim by making their tail move up and down. Manatees use their flippers to steer through the water. They sometimes use their flippers to bring food to their mouths.

◄ Green plants called algae sometimes grow on manatees' backs.

Manatee Range Map

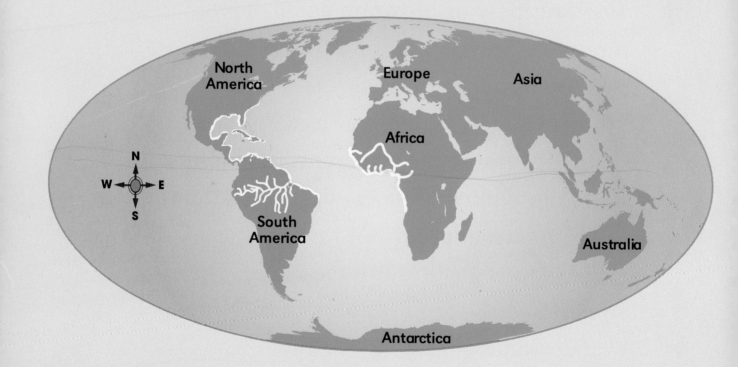

North America

Europe

Asia

Africa

South America

Australia

Antarctica

N
W E
S

Where Manatees Live

Manatees in the World

Manatees live in warm waters close to the equator. Florida manatees live along Florida's Atlantic coast. Antillean manatees swim in coastal areas along the Gulf of Mexico and the Caribbean Sea. West African manatees are found only along the west coast of Africa. Amazonian manatees live in rivers in South America.

Manatee Habitats

Manatees live in shallow water. They rarely travel into water deeper than 10 feet (3 meters). But because of their size, manatees must be in water at least 3 feet (1 meter) deep. Their **habitats** are usually coastal waters, bays, and slow-moving rivers.

Manatees **migrate** when the water gets colder than 68 degrees Fahrenheit (20 degrees Celsius). They travel to warmer waters during the winter months.

◀ A manatee swims along the bank of a shallow river.

What Manatees Eat

Manatees are **herbivores**. They eat both saltwater plants and freshwater plants. They graze on floating plants, sea grasses, and grasses that grow along rivers.

A manatee's mouth is made for eating plants. It has a large upper lip that can pull and tear plants easily. The manatee also has strong teeth in the back of its mouth for grinding plants.

◄ Manatees are sometimes called sea cows. Like cows, they eat only plants.

The Life Cycle of a Manatee

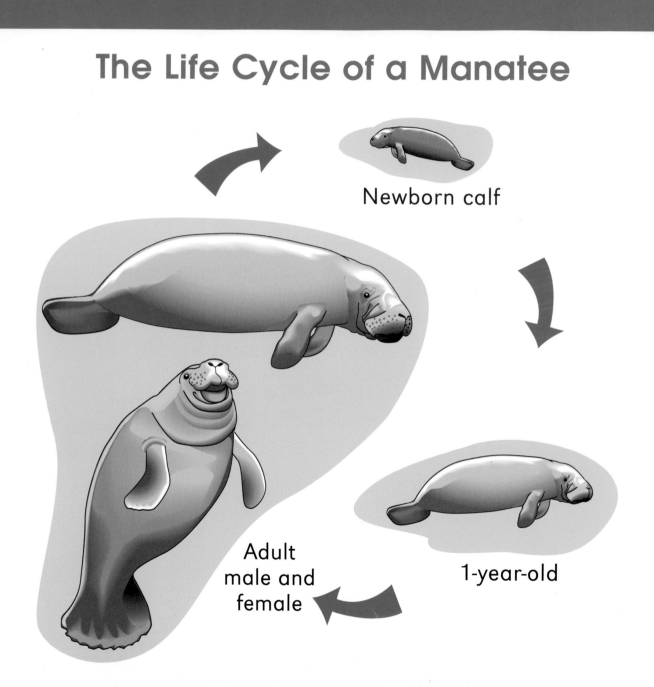

Newborn calf

1-year-old

Adult
male and
female

14

Producing Young

Manatees may **mate** at any time of year. Female manatees often mate with more than one male.

A female gives birth to a calf about 12 months after mating. Most calves are born during the spring or early summer. Manatee calves swim to the surface of the water as soon as they are born.

Growing Up

Newborn manatees look like adult manatees but smaller. They weigh 60 to 70 pounds (27 to 32 kilograms) at birth. They measure about 4 feet (1.2 meters) long.

Manatee calves drink milk from their mothers for about a year. A few weeks after their birth, calves add plants to their diet. Manatee calves stay with their mothers for about two years.

◄ Female manatees teach their calves everything they need to know to survive on their own.

Dangers to Manatees

People can cause great danger to manatees. Manatees live in shallow water and are slow swimmers. Boats sometimes strike and kill them. Many manatees have scars on their backs from boats. People also harm manatees by **polluting** or destroying their habitat.

Florida manatees are **endangered**. Only about 3,000 of these animals are left. People study manatees and their habitats to find ways to protect them.

◀ Members of a wildlife group help a manatee that has been hit by a boat.

Amazing Facts about Manatees

- Manatees have toenails on their flippers. Scientists think the toenails are left over from thousands of years ago, when manatees were land animals.
- A manatee can eat up to 150 pounds (68 kilograms) of food in one day.
- Manatees usually come up for air every 3 to 5 minutes. They can stay underwater for up to 20 minutes.
- Mother manatees can hear their calves' cries from 200 feet (61 meters) away.

◀ Manatees have three or four toenails on each flipper.

Glossary

aquatic (uh-KWAT-ik)—living or growing in water

endangered (en-DAYN-jurd)—at risk of dying out

habitat (HAB-uh-tat)—the place and natural conditions where an animal lives

herbivore (HUR-buh-vor)—an animal that eats plants

mammal (MAM-uhl)—a warm-blooded animal that has a backbone; female mammals feed milk to their young.

mate (MAYT)—to join together to produce young

migrate (MYE-grate)—to move from one area to another

pollute (puh-LOOT)—to make dirty

warm-blooded (warm-BLUHD-id)—having a body temperature that stays the same

Read More

Fink Martin, Patricia A. *Manatees.* A True Book. New York: Children's Press, 2002.

Richardson, Adele D. *Manatees: Peaceful Plant-Eaters.* The Wild World of Animals. Mankato, Minn.: Bridgestone Books, 2003.

Internet Sites

FactHound offers a safe, fun way to find Internet sites related to this book. All of the sites on FactHound have been researched by our staff.

Here's how:
1. Visit *www.facthound.com*
2. Type in this special code **0736843116** for age-appropriate sites. Or enter a search word related to this book for a more general search.
3. Click on the **Fetch It** button.

FactHound will fetch the best sites for you!

Index